RUTH
A Life of Loyalty

A BIBLE STUDY
BY
RUTHANN RIDLEY

NAVPRESS
A MINISTRY OF THE NAVIGATORS
P.O. BOX 6000, COLORADO SPRINGS, COLORADO 80934

5,95

The Navigators is an international Christian organization. Jesus Christ gave His followers the Great Commission to go and make disciples (Matthew 28:19). The aim of The Navigators is to help fulfill that commission by multiplying laborers for Christ in every nation.

NavPress is the publishing ministry of The Navigators. NavPress publications are tools to help Christians grow. Although publications alone cannot make disciples or change lives, they can help believers learn biblical discipleship, and apply what they learn to their lives and ministries.

Cover art: Robert Grace

Printed in the United States of America

CONTENTS

But all of us who are Christians . . .
reflect like mirrors the glory of the
Lord. We are transformed in ever
increasing splendour into His own
image, and this is the work of the
Lord who is the Spirit.

(2 Corinthians 3:18, PH)

AUTHOR

When RuthAnn Ridley was studying music at Baylor University, a friend taught her how to read and study the Bible in a way that made it come alive. For the first time, RuthAnn experienced the power of the Word of God in her daily life. She wanted to help others discover the riches in the Bible, so she began leading Bible studies on a one-to-one basis while still in college. She has never stopped.

RuthAnn graduated Magna Cum Laude with a degree in music. She teaches piano, enjoys reading good literature, and is interested in encouraging Christian artists. She has had articles published in several Christian magazines and has given seminars on "Creativity," "A Biblical Philosophy of Time," "Maintaining the Basics of the Christian Life," and "Woman: A Stumbling Identity."

With her husband, a medical doctor, RuthAnn has led studies for high schoolers, collegians, and neighbors for twenty years. The Ridleys are now ministering with doctors and their wives in Colorado Springs, Colorado, where they live with their three children.

A WORD OF EXPLANATION

In order to fill in the daily lives of the characters in this study, the narratives at the beginning and the end of each lesson include some fictional elements. However, everything is based on thorough research and an understanding of the times.

THE CRISIS

Loyalty isn't loyalty until it's tested.

Two women were walking along a dusty road talking. There was a pause, and then the younger woman said, "You know, Ruth, I don't really know much about you. What's it like in Moab? Why did you decide to come to Bethlehem?"

The other woman looked at her friend and shook her head. "It's a long story."

"I've only heard bits and pieces. Tell me everything."

Ruth's eyes lit up, and she stopped. They walked to a tree, sat down, and made themselves comfortable in the shade. Then Ruth began her story.

"I grew up in Moab and never dreamed I would call any other place home. Moab is a high pasture land riddled with canyons. Some of them, like the River Arnon, are as much as 5,000 feet deep. The capital city is Kir-hareseth. It's built on a long narrow mountain plateau that rises at least 4,000 feet above the Dead Sea. The valleys between the surrounding hills are so deep that the trip to the city always made me tired, but it was exciting.

"I grew up hearing all kinds of stories about the Israelites and their judges. One story was about a fat Moabite king named Eglon who captured the Israelite city of Jericho. The city was a prize

because it gave Moab access to the Jordan valley. Eglon reigned there for eighteen years, and then one day an Israelite judge named Ehud tricked him to get him alone and then stabbed him in his own throne room. After that Moab had to retreat to its original boundaries.

"The more I heard about the Israelites, the more I sensed there was something unusual about them, something real and powerful.

"Another story was about the time the Israelites camped on the plains of Moab. There were at least a million of them. The multitude and the strange cloud that hovered over them scared the king of Moab. So he hired a priest named Balaam to curse the Israelites.

"Balaam kept trying to curse them, but words of blessing would come out instead.

"That story means a lot to me because the turning point of my life was a curse, a curse God turned into a blessing. It all started when Naomi's husband, Elimelech, decided to move his family to Moab."

♋ ♋ ♋

1. Read the entire book of Ruth, and underline the verses that seem to have special significance.

Now let's get a better understanding of the times in which Ruth lived by studying . . .

THE SETTING
2. What dates have been given for when this book was written? (Check notes in your Bible or a reference book.)

3. Read Judges 2 and 3, and describe the general conditions in Israel during this period of history.

4. What are the main events in Ruth 1?

Let's look more closely at the crises Naomi faced, starting with . . .

THE FAMINE
5. Famines were often caused by too much rain, not enough rain, hailstorms, locusts, siege, or invasion. The word *famine* is not found in the book of Judges. However, Judges 6:1-8 describes a time of oppression in which crops were destroyed year after year. Read this passage and describe the nature of the oppression and the Israelites' response.

6. a. Why do you think the Midianite oppression might or might not have been the time of famine referred to in Ruth?

   b. What might Naomi have experienced before she came to Moab? (Judges 6:2-6)

7. Circle the trials Ruth's mother-in-law experienced:

Death of husband
Failing health
Forced to leave home
Infertility
Loneliness
Long hours of labor in the fields
Loss of children
Loss of a friend
Possible starvation
Rebellious children

Sometimes we suffer so much that we begin to lose hope. But Naomi had someone to lean on . . .

THE FRIEND
  8. a. How would you describe Naomi's attitudes about her future and about God at this time? (Ruth 1:12-14,19-21)

  b. The Hebrew word for "afflicted" is *raa*. It means "acted wickedly, brought disaster, damaged, hostile, treated harshly." Empty (*reqam*) can mean "without cause."
     What added insight have the meanings of these words given you about Naomi?

  9. a. How did Ruth respond to Naomi during this time of crisis? (Ruth 1:15-18)

b. Do you think Naomi was normally a bitter, hostile person? Why or why not?

10. Madame Jeanne Guyon was a seventeenth-century Christian who was imprisoned in the Bastille in 1698 for her religious beliefs. John Wesley said of her, "We may search many centuries before we find another woman who was such a pattern of true holiness."[1]

    She began her journeys as an "apostle for inner holiness" when she was thirty-four years old. Church leaders became jealous of her increasing popularity and finally had her arrested as a heretic.

    A maidservant whom Madame Guyon had led to Christ stayed with her in prison. Others continued to slander Madame Guyon, but this servant refused to say one unfavorable word, even though it might have gained her her freedom. She died in the Bastille before her mistress was released.

    a. Has your relationship with someone ever been challenged by a crisis in their lives? If so, what was the situation: persecution, financial struggles, an illness, a loss, a difficult move?

    b. How did you respond?

c. Even if you haven't experienced this yourself, what have you observed about the way others respond to major changes in their friends' or relatives' attitudes or situations?

d. Look up the word *loyalty* in a dictionary, and record the part of the definition that helps you most.

e. A good summary verse for this chapter might be Proverbs 17:17. Read this verse, and rewrite it below in your own words.

Knowing the exact time in history when an event took place can help us understand why people did what they did. Questions 2, 3, 5, and 6 help you uncover information on the historical background of the book of Ruth. Researching the cultural setting of a biblical book or character will prevent faulty interpretation and deepen your understanding of how God works. You can research your own questions about background by using a Bible concordance to guide you to cross-references on customs, countries, etc. Study Bibles and other reference books can provide helpful background information.

§ § §

"I can't imagine Naomi being bitter like that," said Ruth's friend.
"I couldn't either at first. I had always thought of her as a kind of impregnable fortress, like the garrisons on the southern borders of

Moab that had protected us so often. She was the one we went to with our problems.

"Then when Mahlon and Kilion died, Naomi seemed to change. She kept lashing out at God and talking about how He had damaged her and dealt wickedly with her. She didn't seem like the same person. I was afraid for her. She had always been there for me when I needed a friend. How could I let her go back to Bethlehem alone?"

8 8 8

Loyalty is . . . love, in spite of. It refuses to retreat when the battle becomes difficult.

NOTE
1. Edith Deen, *Great Women of the Christian Faith* (Chappaqua, N.Y.: Christian Herald Books, 1959), page 130.

THE VOW

> The man who makes a vow makes an
> appointment with himself at some
> distant time or place.
>
> G.K. CHESTERTON

R ead Ruth 1:8-19. Verse 19 says that Naomi and Ruth *"went on* until they came to Bethlehem."* We have no way of knowing whether they went north or south. If they traveled north, Ruth may have shared something like this with her friend:

         8 8 8

"Naomi told me she felt we should follow the desert road back to Judah, but I insisted on taking the King's Highway. We were in no hurry, and being sure of finding water seemed more important to me than avoiding the Arnon Valley.

"Normally Naomi would have been the one to pray before we began our journey, but she was too depressed. So I prayed silently and asked Jehovah to protect us from wild animals and robbers.

"We passed barley fields that were almost ready for harvest. Many of the green slopes were dotted with sheep, like flecks of white grain. On the second day we began the descent into the Arnon Valley. The slopes looked like giant gray anthills overlapping one another for miles. We spent the night on the floor of the canyon and made our ascent the next day. Then we turned west.

"When we sighted the snow-capped peak of Mount Nebo, Naomi broke her silence. 'It was from that mountain that Moses saw the Promised Land for the first and last time,' she said. 'From its summit they say the land looks like a map west and north. You can see the Great Sea, the long Jordan valley, and the river plain, backed by the Judean hills.'

"Naomi refused to say more. I kept my eyes on the mountain as we walked through the foothills, wishing I could view my new home from its summit. For the first time I felt a spark of hope."

§ § §

If Ruth and Naomi had traveled south, Ruth's account would have been quite different. She might have said:

§ § §

"Naomi was weak and aging, so I decided we should take the southern route to Bethlehem, following the King's Highway through Kirhareseth and avoiding the Wadi Hasa. Much of the journey through Moab was pleasant. The pink blossoms of almond trees often delighted us as we came around a curve.

"But crossing the badlands of the Arabah was another story. It took us two days. The rocks had such bizarre shapes that they scared me when I woke in the middle of the night.

"Once we were almost trapped in a flash flood. It had begun raining, and before we realized what was happening, water was swirling around our feet. We scrambled to higher ground and watched the water rush by. We stood there shivering for a long time.

"Toward the end of the journey, when we were running out of water in the Negev, we longed for the rain we had fled from before. I watched for any sign of wet soil that might indicate the presence of the shallow wells called 'temileh.' When I found one, Naomi would wait as I scraped the mud with a stick and then filled our flasks with the water that seeped out and formed little pools.

"After four days and nights, we finally reached the first of the Judean hills. The slopes were filled with vines and olive trees. We were so relieved to be out of the desert that we both cried."

§ § §

THE TERRAIN
For a better understanding of the geography, refer to the map below.

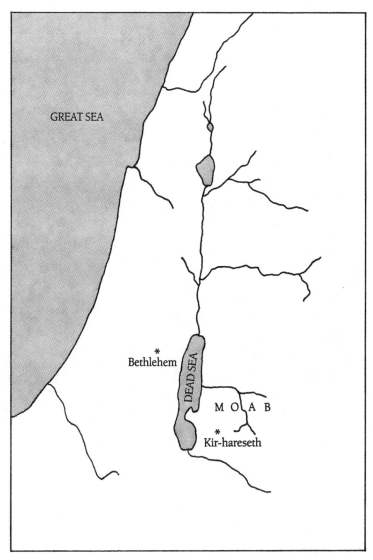

1. Using the maps in the back of your Bible (or a Bible atlas, if you wish), locate and label as many of the following as you can. (Use the map on page 21 for your labeling.)

   a. The Arabah
   b. Israel
   c. Jebus (later Jerusalem)
   d. Jericho
   e. Jordan River
   f. Mount Nebo
   g. Negev Desert
   h. River Arnon
   i. Wadi Hasa

2. Why do you think Ruth wanted to return to Bethlehem with Naomi? (Consider Ruth 1:15 and 2:12.)

Perhaps there were reasons why Ruth shouldn't go to Bethlehem. She may have known . . .

THE RISK
3. Read Deuteronomy 23:3-6. What hint does this passage give about Naomi's thinking when she urged Ruth to stay in Moab?

4. Read Numbers 22:1-25:5 for a better understanding of the relationship between Moab and Israel. Match the following facts and names.

   a. King of Moab   ____ Kariath Huzoth
   b. Balaam   ____ Bamoth Baal
   c. Tried to convince Balaam to   ____ Angel of the Lord
      curse the Israelites.   ____ Where Balak met Balaam
   d. Told Balaam to go with the   ____ ____ Israelites
      Moabites.   ____ Balak

e. Saw the angel of the Lord.
f. Was angry with Balaam.
g. A Moabite town on the Arnon border
h. Where Balak sacrificed cattle and sheep
i. Place where Balaam stood and viewed Israelites
j. Built seven altars.
k. People who rise like a lioness
l. Joined in worshiping Baal.
m. Filled with dread.

___ Princes of Moab
___ God
___ Son of Beor
___ Donkey
___ Lived in Pethor near the river.
___ Moab

5. If you have access to a Bible handbook or Bible dictionary, discover what you can about the Canaanite gods Ruth's people worshiped.

Three figures stand in the middle of the road. They walk a few steps, then stop, looking back the way they came, weeping and talking quietly to one another in urgent tones about . . .

THE DECISION
6. List the action words in Ruth 1:14-19.

7. Which action words are repeated?

8. Which words are the most intense?

The Hebrew word for "clung" is *dabaq*. It means "to cleave, hold fast, closely pursue, be deeply attracted."

9. a. How many times do the words *you* or *your* appear in verses 16-17?

b. What was Ruth's focus in her vow?

10. Ruth believed in Naomi. She understood her mother-in-law's misery and determined to be her friend and to help in whatever way she could. Naomi owed her daughter-in-law much.

The great composer Franz Schubert owed the productivity of his creative life to the loyalty of friends. Because his father didn't consider composing music a valid profession, Schubert was educated to be a school teacher. He taught for three miserable years.

When his friend Schober observed the physical and emotional strain Schubert was experiencing, Schober offered Schubert a place to live free of charge. Other friends of the musician found appliances, bought meals, provided paper for composing, and gave encouragement on a daily basis.

Schubert was able to quit teaching and give his life to composing. Today, music critics call Schubert "the greatest writer of songs and one of the supreme creators of melody."[1]

If Schubert had not had friends who were *there for him* at the right time, we might not have his music today.

a. Most of us are familiar with Ruth's vow because we hear it in marriage ceremonies. Originally, however, it was a vow between friends. Should we make vows to friends today? Why or why not?

b. What have you learned about friendship in this lesson that you would like to apply to your life?

This lesson focuses on the geographical setting of the book of Ruth. A study of terrain through the use of maps and atlases will often make a Bible story come alive.

§ § §

Ruth's friend was silent for a moment. Then she asked, "Do you think a woman Naomi's age would have made it alone?"

"I'm not sure. I had to force her to eat. If the fire went out at night, she never made a move to start it again. She didn't seem to care if she froze to death, and sometimes she had trouble getting her breath in the middle of the night.

"This scared me, and my grief and fear would take over. But then I would pull myself together, pray, and try to comfort her. Once I remember throwing my shawl over her shaking body and telling her that two were better than one—that together we would find a reason for living.

"She still didn't respond."

§ § §

Loyalty is . . . a "going back with," instead of a "turning back from." It is being available to a friend, being there, wherever "there" is.

NOTE
Opening quotation is from *The Quotable Chesterton.*
1. Jane Stuart Smith and Betty Carlson, *A Gift of Music* (Westchester, Ill.: Good News Publishers, 1978), page 105.

THE DAILIES

Faithfulness may be measured best in
the routine duties of a day.

*R*uth and her friend got up and stretched for a moment. They
were about half a mile from Bethlehem and could see its gates
from where they stood.

"Had Naomi told you much about Bethlehem before you
arrived?"

"She told me it was in the hill country of Judea not far from
Jebus. When I first saw it, the slopes were dotted with flowering
almond trees. The peppery smell of the blossoms followed us as we
climbed to the gates of the city. It made me think of home.

"When the people recognized Naomi and came over to us, I
realized how awful I looked. My sandals were muddy, and my skirt
was torn. I waited, but Naomi didn't think to introduce me to her
friends. I felt so alone.

"Naomi had been in Moab for a long time, and everybody was
excited to see her again. Somebody offered to give her a place to stay.

"We did little but sleep and eat for several days. People were
very generous, but we didn't wait long to discuss how we could keep
from being totally dependent. I suggested that I glean in the barley
fields after the crops were harvested. I thought it was the least I
could do.

"When I left the house on my first day of work, I was glad to be alone. I needed some time to think. But as I walked down to the fields, the strangeness of the countryside and the crude huts made me feel cold. I was a foreigner."

§ § §

Let's see what it was like to work all day in . . .

A BARLEY FIELD

1. Read Ruth 2 and divide the chapter into sections. What title can you think of for each section?

2. Circle the best definition for "gleaning."

   - Threshing someone else's crops
   - Transplanting seedlings
   - Harvesting
   - Collecting the remaining grain
   - Separating the grain from the chaff

3. What else can you learn about gleaning from Leviticus 19:9-10 and Deuteronomy 24:19?

4. Record all the words in the second chapter of Ruth that refer to work.

5. What do verses 7, 17, and 23 tell us about the quality of Ruth's work?

After she had worked for awhile, Boaz came striding across the fields, and spoke to her as though he understood her feelings. Was it just . . .

A CHANCE ENCOUNTER?
6. What words does Ruth use to describe the way Boaz ministered to her? (Ruth 2:10,13)

The Hebrew word for *kindly* or its equivalent in verse 13 is *leb*. It means "inner man, heart, concern." The *New American Standard Bible* translates verse 13 as, "You have spoken to my heart."

7. What different emotions or moods do you notice in this chapter?

8. Look through the chapter and decide what verses might be considered key verses. Record the references here.

9. In his book *The Baronet's Song*, George MacDonald tells of a poor family who only had a few flowers, a small field of oats, one of potatoes, and a few stalks of cabbage and kale. The children were grown and worked in the village. But they loved to come home on the weekends. The meal their

mother would make for them would never be elaborate, but they were in agreement that "the porridge was such as none but mother's cow could yield, the cakes such as she only could bake. . . . Simplest things will carry the result of honest attention as plainly as more elaborate dishes."[1]

Ruth's gleaning could be compared to the routine of daily housekeeping: cooking, mending, washing, picking up toys, taking out trash. These chores seem unending. They require diligence and are notoriously unglamorous, but they give our families a sense of security.

a. List the tasks you have trouble doing well on an everyday basis.

b. Being faithful in small things can mean a great deal to other people. Some examples:

- Being on time
- Being willing to retype a letter or rewash a shirt
- Making the phone call you promised you would make
- Picking up a tube of toothpaste on the way home

Add some of your own ideas to this list and mark the ones you would like to work on.

Questions 4, 5, 7, and 8 in this lesson can help you learn to observe. *Observation* is a Bible study technique that asks the question, "What does it say?" not "What does it mean?" This is the most important part of accurate Bible study. Be sure you don't try to make the text say something it really doesn't say. Test your observation skills by answering this question: Does this book say that Boaz and Ruth fell in love?

§ § §

"I wouldn't have been willing to do what you did, Ruth."

"Gleaning was hard work, but it was the best way I could think
of to help Naomi. The first morning was the worst. I could see the
hills of Moab from Boaz's fields. They made me long for the sounds
and smells of Kir-hareseth. Besides that, I knew the other girls were
talking about me.

"Then I met Boaz, and everything changed. He called me
'daughter' and mentioned how difficult it must have been for me to
leave my parents and come to live with a people I didn't know.

"He sensed how humiliated I was by the comments of the men
in the fields and told them not to talk to me like that. I felt as though
Boaz had reached inside of me and touched something no one had
ever touched before.

"After he left, I began to find even more stalks than before. At
the end of the day I had to thresh what I had gleaned so I could carry
it home. I gathered over half a bushel!

"Naomi met me at the door with all kinds of questions. After I
told her what had happened, she was full of praise for God and Boaz.
That's the way she had always been in the past: quick to notice
God's hand in circumstances and quick to notice the good in others.

"And me? I didn't even think about being afraid as I walked
home in the dark. It was at least a mile, but the night breeze was
cool on my face. The sky sparkled. And I was busy singing praises to
God."

§ § §

Loyalty is … a daily commitment. It
may mean working hard to keep
someone alive emotionally, spiritually,
and even physically. This kind of
constancy reflects the character of
God.

NOTE
1. George MacDonald, *The Baronet's Song* (Minneapolis, Minn.: Bethany House Publishers, 1983), page 76.

THE RENDEZVOUS

Only a life lived for others is a
life worthwhile.
ALBERT EINSTEIN

*R*uth's young friend was excited. "When did you and Boaz begin
to think about getting married?"

"I gleaned in his fields until the end of June, and then Boaz and
his men began spending almost every night at the threshing floor.
I found myself thinking about Boaz more and more. Each night I
would imagine him bringing in the sheaves from the fields and putting them on the hard-packed clay floors. I could almost see oxen
dragging the studded wooden boards behind them as they trampled
the grain. Boaz had explained to me that the reason they winnowed
at night was to take advantage of the night breezes.

"One night Naomi said, 'I've been thinking about you and
Boaz, and I have a plan.'"

§ § §

NAOMI'S PLAN

1. Read Ruth 3, and write a short summary of the events.

2. Record any questions you have about the text. Bombard each paragraph with as many "how, what, why, where, and when" questions as you can think of.

Example: *What is winnowing?*
Why did Naomi tell Ruth to go to Boaz in the middle of the night?

After the threshing was done, laborers "winnowed" the grain by tossing it into the air with a wooden fork or shovel so the wind could blow away the chaff.

3. a. Why do you think Ruth trusted Naomi so completely?

b. What qualities do you see in Naomi in this chapter? (verses 1,3,18)

4. Read verses 5-6, and note whether the following statements are true or false.

____ Ruth did everything Naomi asked after making sure she understood her mother-in-law's reasoning.
____ Ruth followed Naomi's instructions down to the last detail.
____ Ruth did most of what Naomi asked.
____ Ruth considered Naomi's plan overnight and then did what she asked.

Naomi probably knew Boaz well enough to predict what he would do. She could anticipate . . .

BOAZ'S RESPONSE

5. What did Boaz understand Ruth to mean when she said, "Spread the corner of your garment over me"? (See Ezekiel 16:8.)

6. a. One of the themes of the book of Ruth is kindness. Explain the "kindness" that Boaz considered so great in verse 10. Refer to different translations if you wish.

b. Look for other verses in the book of Ruth that contain some form of the word *kindness,* and record the verses (or phrases) below.

7. Read Ruth 4:21 and Matthew 1:5. Who were Boaz's mother and father? (Refer to Joshua 2:1-21,6:17 for more details about Boaz's mother.)

Salmon would have married Boaz's mother sometime after the fall of Jericho. By the time the Israelites had experienced the cycles of war and peace recorded in Judges, and Naomi had spent ten years in Moab, a son of Salmon's would have been at least forty years old.

Ruth is called a young woman or girl in chapter 2 (*maarah:*

girl, maiden). This noun usually refers to a marriageable but unmarried girl. It emphasizes the youthfulness of the girl and indicates . . .

RUTH'S EXCELLENCE
8. Let's take a closer look at Ruth's character. What words are used to describe her in Ruth 3:10-11?

9. The word translated "excellent" in the NASB and "noble character" in the NIV is the Hebrew word *chayil*. It means "strength, wealth, riches, army, capable, valiant, or force."
    The following references give examples of different translations of the Hebrew word *chayil*. Record the examples below.

Exodus 18:25

Ruth 2:1

1 Samuel 9:1

1 Kings 1:42

Proverbs 31:10

10. In what ways does Ruth's life reflect the principles in Philippians 2:3-4?

11. Anna was a twentieth-century woman who also put other people's interests above her own. She lived in a country where conditions were continually growing worse. There were fewer and fewer freedoms, and most people had to work at least twelve hours a day. Practically everyone was undernourished because staples, meat, and eggs were rationed or nonexistent.

There was little joy in life.

A few people in one village, however, had an inner joy everybody noticed. Anna was one of these people. They were all Christians.

Anna loved her country despite its discomforts, and she knew her people were becoming more and more open to the gospel. When she was given a chance to leave and make her home in another country, she refused.

She decided to stay because she felt her people needed her.

We know little about this kind of deprivation in the West. Our society is a "me" society that does everything it can to eliminate discomfort and pain. Loyalty is rare because it requires sacrifice.

• Loyalty to a sick parent may mean giving up your own comfort and freedom.
• Loyalty to a spouse may involve leaving your home or your job and putting effort into a dream that is not your own.
• Loyalty to a friend may mean risking your reputation.

a. Do you have any dreams or desires that conflict with the needs of someone who needs your loyalty? Explain.

b. Even if the answer to the previous question is "No," write a few sentences about ways you might put somebody's interests above your own in the future.

Questions 2, 3, 5, and 6 in this lesson encourage you to ask *questions* that will help you interpret the meaning behind the story. If some of the questions you listed still haven't been answered when you have completed this lesson, try looking up cross-references, referring to other translations, or using a commentary.

§ § §

"It all seems so romantic when you tell it, but I would have been awfully afraid if I were you."

"I was! I would never have risked my reputation the way I did that night if anyone other than Naomi had told me to do it, and I wasn't even sure I wanted to marry Boaz. But Naomi loved me as much as I loved her, and I knew I could count on her wisdom.

"I watched the red-gold sun as it sank and then walked to the threshing floor. The stench of oxen mingled with the odor of beer. I hid and looked for Boaz among the men. Then I watched him until he left the jugs and went off alone to sleep beside a pile of grain.

"After he fell asleep, I crept toward him, lifted his loose-fitting cloak, and lay down at his feet. The wool should have kept me warm. but I trembled for a long time.

"Even after talking to Boaz, I was afraid. I had many fears. There was the fear that someone would see me and think the wrong

thing, and the fear that Boaz would not be able to marry me: that I would have to marry the nearer kinsman instead.

"Everything was uncertain that summer. The days were filled with many kinds of fears. All three of us felt it."

§ § §

Loyalty is ... focusing on the other person—being willing to set aside our personal desires.

THE REWARD

Blessings ever wait on virtuous deeds,
and though late, a sure
reward succeeds.
CONGREVE

"*B*oaz *must have gone to the main gate to finalize the arrange-ments for your marriage. Did our customs seem strange to you?" the young friend asked.*

"No, they really didn't seem strange at all. Your city govern-ments are similar to ours. The men of Moab do their business and their legal transactions at the main gate, just as you do. All of our major decisions are made by the elders: military commanders and men who are over sixty years of age. I knew that it was the same way here.

"I'm sure people wondered when they saw Boaz at the gate so early in the morning. . . . All I could do was wait and pray. I threw myself into the bread making and cooked the porridge. I tried to spend as little time as possible watching for Boaz to come back and tell me what happened.

"Naomi promised me I could depend on him, and she was right. He was determined to settle the issue of our marriage that day."

§ § §

Boaz was a faithful . . .

KINSMAN-REDEEMER
1. Read Ruth 4. Which verse do you think captures the main idea of the chapter?

2. How many references to redemption can you find in the fourth chapter of Ruth? List them here.

3. What is a recurring concern you notice in verses 5,10,11, and 14?

4. What can you find out about the duties of a kinsman-redeemer from other verses in the Bible, such as Leviticus 25:48-49, Deuteronomy 25:5-8, and Nehemiah 5:8? (You may also want to use the cross-references in your Bible, or use a concordance.)

5. If you would like to know more about Boaz's background, reread Ruth 4:18-22. Then read Genesis 38, 46:12, and 49:10. Note interesting facts below.

Consider God's response to Ruth's faithfulness. She experienced His . . .

BLESSINGS AND REWARDS
  6. Read the following verses and complete the chart below.

WHAT WE NEED TO DO	WHAT GOD PROMISES
Proverbs 21:21	
Hosea 10:12	
Galatians 6:7-9	
Hebrews 6:10	

7. What is the main message of the following verses?

  1 Corinthians 15:58

  Hebrews 10:35-36

8. What rewards did Ruth receive for her loyalty? (Consider Ruth 4:18-22. Note 2:5,11 for an example of reaping what you sow.)

9. What good wishes or blessings did the townspeople express toward Boaz, Ruth, and Naomi? (Ruth 4:11,14-15)

10. What similar blessings can you find in chapters 1-3?

This short book contains thirteen blessings, giving the reader the feel of prophecy or proclamation. Ruth's story is a story of tragedy and hardship, but it is also a witness to the faithfulness of God.

Now in our last look at Naomi we see . . .

A TRANSFORMED LIFE
11. Why do you think the book begins and ends with Naomi? (Ruth 1:1-5, 4:14-17)

12. Describe the changes you see in Naomi as the story progresses.

13. Helen Keller was blind and deaf from the time she was two years old. She made her family's life miserable with tantrums and demands. When she was almost seven, her parents found a teacher for her named Anne Sullivan.

Helen was an extremely difficult pupil, but Anne persevered until she discovered a way to communicate with her pupil. From that point on, Helen was a different person. Anne taught her to read Braille, and later Helen learned to speak. Anne stayed with Helen and accompanied her to Radcliffe College to interpret lectures and class discussions.

After Anne died, Helen traveled extensively, lecturing on the behalf of the blind in underdeveloped and war-ravaged countries. She wrote eight books that have been translated into fifty languages and brought new courage to millions.

Anne Sullivan was rewarded for her loyalty by the dramatic change and productivity in her pupil's life.

a. Ruth was rewarded in her lifetime with a husband and a son and beyond her lifetime by a descendant who became king. Does God promise we will always see the rewards of loyalty in this life?

b. How do God's promises in questions 6 and 7 affect your outlook on your relationships at this time?

The best commentary on the Bible is the Bible itself. Questions 4-7 focus on *cross-referencing* to broaden your understanding of characters and themes. To find your own cross-references, use the concordance in the back of a study Bible or a separate, exhaustive concordance

§ § §

"Naomi really loved you, didn't she? She wanted you to feel secure."

"I think Naomi spent many years looking for a home. She and her husband sought refuge in Moab, and the prosperity we were experiencing made them feel secure. But after Mahlon and Kilion died, she began to think of Bethlehem as her home.

"When she came out of her depression, she was concerned that I have a home and a reliable husband. I'll always be grateful for the way she helped me appeal to Boaz. But I think the truth is that Naomi and I found a home in each other. No matter where we traveled, we would have been home, if we were together."

§ § §

Loyalty is . . . a quiet, almost hidden virtue. It means being faithful in difficult times, making daily sacrifices, putting someone's need above our own. A loyal friend can change the course of a person's life. God will never fail to reward us for this quality.

NOTE
Opening quotation is from *The New Dictionary of Thoughts.*

GOD'S LOYALTY— HIS FAITHFULNESS

May I never fail to retreat to Him ...
the friend that loveth at all times,
who is touched with the feeling
of my infirmities.

The Valley of Vision
a collection of Puritan prayers

A ll of us long for unconditional love: loyalty from a spouse,
no matter how we act; the faithful companionship of a
friend, no matter what we reveal. But such loyalty is rare.

Ruth's legendary faithfulness won her an exalted place in
history.

The Apostle Peter says that all who love God have a
chance to participate in the divine nature (2 Peter 1:4). God is
in the process of conforming us to His image.

It is this image that Ruth reflected in such a powerful way.
God is the source of all faithfulness.

In the beginning was God, and one of the most essential
parts of His character is faithfulness. We see this in . . .

THE UNCHANGING LOVE OF GOD
  1. Read 2 Chronicles 5:11-14 and try to accurately visualize
     the scene.

     a. Who were the characters?

b. What musical instruments did they use?

c. Describe the place.

d. For what did the worshipers praise God?

2. The "lovingkindness" of God is referred to at least 150 times in the Old Testament. The Hebrew word (*chesed*) is rich with several layers of meaning: "Deeds of devotion, faithfulness, loyal deeds, loyalty, mercies, unchanging love." It is the same word translated *kindness* in reference to Ruth (Ruth 3:10).
   In the above definition of "lovingkindness," what words show us that God's love is a love that takes action?

3. a. What different names are given to Jesus Christ in Revelation 19:11-16? Note which name is placed first.

   b. What is the final quality mentioned in Isaiah's description of Christ? (Isaiah 11:1-5)

The belt or sash worn by people in Bible times was either cloth or leather and was worn over a loose coat-like shirt. . . . [The leather belt or girdle was from] two to six inches wide, and was frequently studded with iron, silver, or gold. It was worn by soldiers, by men of the desert, and by countrymen who . . . engaged in the rougher pursuits of life. When one was to walk or run, or enter into any type of service he "girded himself" for the journey or the task at hand.[1]

The Lord prepares for service on our behalf by girding Himself with faithfulness.

c. How is God's faithfulness described in Psalm 89:8?

d. What significance does this have for your life?

4. How do the following verses describe God's faithfulness and lovingkindness?

Psalm 36:5-7

Psalm 89:2

Psalm 100:4-5

Psalm 111:7-8 (Note: the NASB uses the word *truth* instead of *faithfulness*.)

Psalm 136:1-9

5. Look up the words *loyalty* and *faithfulness* in a dictionary. What subtle difference in meaning do you find?

6. Because we experience so little perfect loyalty in earthly relationships, we have a basic uncertainty about God's loyalty. Note this uncertainty in Lamentations 3:16-24.

   a. How did the writer deal with his uncertainties?

   b. How can you deal with your misgivings?

7. a. Substitute a dictionary definition for the word *everlasting* in the sentence, "His lovingkindness is everlasting."

   b. Now substitute one of the meanings for "lovingkindness" in the same sentence. (Refer to question 2.)

   c. Create as many sentences as you can using the different meanings of these two words.

      Example: *His unchanging love never comes to an end.*
      His loyal deeds last forever.

8. How can a deeper understanding of God's loyalty help you in your current circumstances?

In every generation, the unfaithfulness of man has stood in stark contrast to the faithfulness of God. He knows . . .

THE CHARACTER OF MAN
9. How does God describe man's loyalty in Hosea 6:4?

10. Read Hosea 11:12 and 2 Timothy 2:13. What contrasts do you see?

MAN	GOD

11. How does the writer of Proverbs describe our sinful tendencies? (Proverbs 20:6, 25:14)

12. What is David's lament in Psalm 12:1?

Yet God remains compassionate toward us. He is mindful that we are but dust.

> I remember my affliction and my wandering,
>   the bitterness and the gall.
> I well remember them,
>   and my soul is downcast within me.
> Yet this I call to mind
>   and therefore I have hope:
> Because of the LORD's great love we are not consumed,
>   for his compassions never fail.
> They are new every morning;
>   great is your faithfulness.
>
> (Lamentations 3:19-23)

NOTE
1. Merrill C. Tenney, ed., *Pictorial Bible Dictionary* (Franklin, Tenn.: Southwestern Company, 1975), page 226.

GOD'S LOYALTY—
HIS COMPASSION

> As one who has sought refuge in
> Christ, I precommit to Him regardless
> of how it may work out; He pre-
> commits to me. . . . God does not
> accept me conditionally, on the basis
> of my projected behavior. He keeps
> [His] vow, and therein is grace.
>
> PHILLIP YANCEY

God is loyal because He is compassionate. He is a God of love. He is there for us in times of crisis and routine, willing to go out of His way to meet our needs, even when we don't deserve it.

God is a dependable refuge for all who believe in His Son. We can experience . . .

GOD'S COMPASSION
  1. What reason does Nehemiah give for God's faithfulness? (Nehemiah 9:31)

The NASB says, "In Thy great compassion Thou didst not make an end of them or forsake them."

  2. How does God react to being rejected by His people? (Hosea 11:7-9)

3. Define the word *compassion* using a dictionary.

It is difficult to understand how a Holy God can be faithful to His people when they sin. We need to realize . . .

WHAT HAPPENS WHEN WE SIN
4. a. Read Psalm 40:11-13. What is happening in David's life when he appeals to God's faithfulness?

   b. How does God demonstrate His faithfulness in Psalm 89:30-34?

5. What two principles recur in each of the following verses? (They are recorded for you here as they appear in the *New American Standard Bible*.)

   I will be a father to him and he will be a son to Me; when he commits iniquity, I will correct him with the rod of men and the strokes of the sons of men, but My lovingkindness shall not depart from him. (2 Samuel 7:14-15)

   He will abide before God forever; appoint lovingkindness and truth, that they may preserve him. (Psalm 61:7)

   Lovingkindness and truth have met together; righteousness and peace have kissed each other. (Psalm 85:10)

   Do not let kindness and truth leave you; bind them around your neck, write them on the tablet of your heart. (Proverbs 3:3)

In Proverbs 3:3, the word *bind* can be translated "league them together." In other words, love your friend, but love him enough to remind him of the truth.

Dostoevski's heroine in the book *Crime and Punishment* seemed disloyal when she convinced the man she loved to turn himself in as a murderer. But then she followed him to prison camp and stayed with him. This is God's kind of loyalty, the kind that combines faithfulness *and* truth.

God's kind of loyalty also involves availability. He is always there for me, ready to meet my deepest needs in times of crisis or routine . . . .

GOD'S AVAILABILITY

6. "Day by day the Lord also pours out his steadfast love upon me, and through the night I sing his songs and pray to God who gives me life" (Psalm 42:8, TLB).

Read the following verses and record God's loyal deeds under the appropriate heading.

Exodus 16:2-4,11-14
2 Kings 20:1-6
Hosea 11:3-4
1 Corinthians 10:13
2 Corinthians 1:3, 7:6-7
2 Thessalonians 3:3
1 John 1:9

DAILY NEEDS	TIMES OF CRISIS

7. a. How can James 1:17 make us more aware of God's faithfulness on a daily basis?

b. What daily gifts does He give us that we tend to take for granted?

God's unfailing love is a mighty refuge, shown to us by . . .

HIS COMFORT

8. What images does the psalmist use to describe the quality of refreshment we find in God? (Psalm 36:7-9)

9. What is the climactic point of Deuteronomy 32:1-4?

When God is referred to as the Rock, two different Hebrew words are used interchangeably. One is *tsur,* which means mountain; the other is *sela,* which means a cleft in a rock or a crag. God provides us with a magnificent source of strength, endurance, and reliability, but He also gives us shelter when we need it.

10. a. Read Psalm 91:1-4 and list other images of God's faithfulness.

b. What is a rampart (verse 4; translated "bulwark" or "buckler" in some versions)? You may need to look these words up in a dictionary.

One morning at 6:00 a.m. a family was wakened by the sound of shattering glass. They went upstairs and found that the high winds, which had been blowing all night, had broken their dining room window. The strong winds continued throughout the day, whipping through that level of the house with no restraint. Papers, baskets, and magazines flew through the air. Plants had to be moved away from the window so they wouldn't be damaged.

We have no idea what the winds would be like if the Lord weren't constantly protecting us. He is like an unyielding storm window, a rock, a rampart who shields us from things we can't even imagine, according to . . .

HIS PROMISES
11. Read the following promises, and write out the ones that mean the most to you at this time in your life.

Psalm 91:14-15
Jeremiah 32:38-41
Romans 8:38-39
Hebrews 10:16-17, 13:5-6

12. God's love is a covenant love. The promises belong to those who seek His refuge, who believe in Him, who love Him, who count Him as the only real God.

    If there is some reason you feel God hasn't kept His promises to you, what help can you find in Hebrews 10:35-36?

13. Choose one of the following activities to conclude your study of God's loyalty:

    • Write a prayer of thanksgiving to God for different aspects of His faithfulness.
    • Review the application questions in lessons 6 (questions 6, 8) and 7 (questions 8, 12), and write a summary of your answers.
    • Choose one or two verses from lessons 6 and 7 to meditate on and/or memorize. Copy them from your favorite translation.

§ § §

A dying man welcomed a visitor to his hospital room. The sick man's daughter watched from a corner as the two men talked. They were at ease with one another, glad to be together. When the visitor left, the daughter said, "He's a good friend, isn't he, Dad?"

The man answered, "Yes, you won't find many like him in a lifetime. Loyal friends are hard to come by."

When we compare the vastness of God's loyalty to the limits of ours, we realize how faithless we are. We will have to have His help, if we are going to be loyal at all.

§ § §

NOTE

Opening quotation is from "Should I Hate Myself or Love Myself?" in *Christianity Today*.

MIRIAM'S DISLOYALTY

God sends no one away empty except
those who are full of themselves.
DWIGHT L. MOODY

**This lesson will help you discover more on your own.
It is for those who have a desire to learn about inductive
Bible study and who would like a challenge.**

*M*iriam was a prophetess, a leader in the nation of Israel; and
Moses was her brother, a man with a mission he wished he
didn't have.

*There were days when Moses carried the burden of leadership
like a mighty song. But not today. The shaft of sadness inside him
was almost unbearable.*

*A few days before, he had been rejoicing in the victory the Lord
was promising Israel as they again set out for Canaan. He felt
hopeful.*

*But everyone had fallen back into the same old cycle: The
people sinned; the Lord's anger burned; and Moses was trapped
between the two.*

*"All they do is whine and complain," Moses thought to himself.
"Sometimes I wish I didn't care."*

*Moses lay in his tent, totally drained after a depression so deep
that he had begged the Lord to kill him. He was raw inside from
the constant criticism of those he only sought to serve. But God
knew.*

§ § §

Consider Miriam's treatment of Moses in the light of what he had just been through.

1. Read Numbers 12. Choose between the following.

   • Write a short paragraph summarizing the events of the chapter.
   • Outline the passage.

EXPLORING THE BACKGROUND

2. Read Exodus 14:29-31, Exodus 15, and Numbers 10-11 for a better understanding of the events that led up to Numbers 12.

   Fill in the following charts:

EXODUS PASSAGES

MAIN EVENTS	GEOGRAPHY	CHARACTERS
Example: *The people of Israel walked through the sea on dry land.*	(refer to a map) Example: *The Red Sea separates the southern part of Egypt from the Sinai Peninsula.*	

EXODUS PASSAGES

MAIN EVENTS	GEOGRAPHY	CHARACTERS

NUMBERS PASSAGES

MAIN EVENTS	GEOGRAPHY AND TIME FRAMES	CHARACTERS
	Example: *They had been gone from Egypt over a year* (Numbers 10:11).	

3. Compare Moses' emotions in Numbers 11:11-15 with those of Naomi in the first chapter of Ruth.

The Israelites seemed to go from one crisis to another. They lived on a roller coaster of emotions. Even Miriam and Aaron were discontent. Let's look at . . .

WHAT MIRIAM DID AND WHY
  4. Read Numbers 12:1-3 and consider the following questions. (Note: As you study the Bible, you will realize that there is always more to discover about any passage or truth. Don't be frustrated by a feeling of not being able to finish every idea or question. Do what you can in the time you have.)

Observations (What does it say?)
  a. Whose name appears first in this account?

  b. What questions does Miriam ask?

  c. Miriam is pitting her leadership against Moses's leadership in a kind of comparison. What other comparisons do you see in these verses?

  d. What words are repeated more than once?

  e. What words or phrases are especially descriptive?

Questions (What does it mean?)
f. The word *spoke* (verse 1) is the Hebrew word *dabar*. It means "proclaimed, counseled, or declared."
    What light does this definition throw on the extent of Miriam's disloyalty?

g. List any questions you have about verses 1-3. (Why, when, what, how, etc.)

Cross-references (What do other Scriptures say?)
h. Read Exodus 2 for more background on Miriam. After considering Exodus 15:20-21 along with Exodus 2, how would you describe Miriam's potential?

i. Choose two of the questions you listed in part g above and find cross-references to answer your questions.

When the Lord heard what Miriam and Aaron had said, He immediately responded. It's important to know . . .

WHAT GOD SAID AND WHY HE SAID IT
5. Read Numbers 12:4-9 and use the following guide for study.

Observations (What does it say?)
a. Describe the nature of God's response to Miriam and Aaron's declaration. (Hint: Note action words.)

b. What words does God use to describe Moses?

c. How would you describe the atmosphere or tone of this passage?

Questions (What does it mean?)
d. Use a dictionary to look up the meaning of two of the following words:

- Prophet
- Riddles
- Servant
- Visions

The Hebrew word for "burned" is *charah*. It means "become furious."

e. How do you think Miriam's ministry was different from Moses' ministry?

Cross-references (What do other Scriptures say?)
f. Use a concordance to find out more about one of the
following:

- God's anger
- Prophets

Conclusions (Putting it all together)
g. Choose one of the following:

- Write a paragraph recreating this portion of the drama
in your own words (Numbers 12:4-9). Include colors,
sounds, and feelings.
- Jot down any thoughts on leadership that come to you
as a result of studying this section.

Miriam's offense was so serious that the Lord didn't stop at a
warning. He issued . . .

THE PUNISHMENT
6. Read Numbers 12:10-16 and complete the following.

Observations (What does it say?)
a. List the words that make this section vivid.

b. To whom does Aaron appeal on Miriam's behalf?

c. How does Aaron describe what he and Miriam had done?

d. What kinds of attitudes do you notice?

Questions (What does it mean?)
e. What do you think could have happened if Miriam had been a positive influence on Aaron?

f. Why is Miriam silent after verse 3?

Cross-references (What do other Scriptures say?)
g. How do you think Exodus 19:9 might relate to the events in Numbers 12?

h. What was the significance of having someone spit in your face? (Deuteronomy 25:9, Job 17:6)

NOTES AND CONCLUSIONS

7. Use the space that follows to record quotes from commentaries, tangent thoughts and ideas, conclusions, and applications.

a. Notes from commentaries:

b. Thoughts:

Example: *What a sobering thing it is to short-circuit God's plan for our lives! Shall we begin well and finish badly?*

c. Conclusions:

Example: *Ruth's loyalty was rewarded. Miriam's disloyalty was punished.*

d. Applications:

Example: *Miriam's criticism added to an already heavy
burden. I need to ask myself if I am guilty of the same thing in
my relationship with my spouse, a close friend, or someone in
authority over me.*

THE SUMMARY

8. When you study a chapter of the Bible, it is helpful to
remember the principle of moving from the whole to the
parts and back to the whole.

We have dissected Numbers 12. Now try putting it
together again by doing one of the following:

- Think of an original title for the chapter.
- Decide on a key verse.
- Capture the main thought in one or two sentences.

NOTE
Opening quotation is from the *Topical Encyclopedia of Living Quotations.*

EPILOGUE

In one of his novels, Thornton Wilder speaks of a man and woman who "lived at one remove from that self that supports the generality of men, the self that is a bundle of . . . greeds, of vanities, and of easily offended pride."[1] Moses's sister, Miriam, never progressed this far. She was greedy and proud.

A loyal woman is one who has given up these tendencies. She puts others' needs above her own and makes herself available even when she receives no praise or appreciation.

She endures change and hurt and weakness, in an effort to lighten inner burdens she may only partially understand. She has learned, as G.K. Chesterton says, that a person who makes a vow truly does make an appointment with herself at a distant time and place.

C.S. Lewis came face to face with this truth because of a promise he once made. Many people questioned his long-term commitment to Mrs. Moore, the mother of a friend who died in the war. He brought her into his home and treated her like his own mother, because he had told his friend he would do so. Mrs. Moore was sharp tongued and unsympathetic. His home life was miserable. Friends criticized him for this eccentric commitment, but he was silent on the matter. His reward lay in the future.

A person who is truly loyal is someone who reflects the unchanging love of God, a love forever intense and concerned, a love that expects the best and endures all things.

In our contemporary culture, loyalty seems outmoded, like something pulled out of a dusty file. It is an ancient virtue with champions like Ruth, whose love was better to Naomi than seven sons, and Jesus of Nazareth who suffered for those He loved and was given the Name that is above all names.

In order to help the truths you have learned in this study become real in your own life, consider memorizing one or more of the following verses. You will probably find it helpful to write the verses you choose on a three-by-five card and tape them in a prominent place.

- Proverbs 17:17
- Proverbs 21:21
- Romans 8:38-39
- 2 Corinthians 3:18
- Galatians 6:9
- Philippians 2:3-4
- 2 Timothy 2:13
- Hebrews 13:5

NOTE
1. Thornton Wilder, *Woman of Andros* (New York: Albert and Charles Boni, 1930), page 86.

BIBLIOGRAPHY

The Archaeological Commentary on the Bible by Gonzalo Baez-
Camargo (Garden City, N.Y.: Doubleday, 1984) is a valu-
able summary of archaeological discoveries, which shed
light on obscure passages of the Bible. One of its unique
factors is the way it is organized. The archaeological
information is gathered and arranged in order, from
Genesis to Revelation, by chapter and verse.

The Bible Almanac, edited by J.I. Packer, Merrill C. Tenney, and
William White (Nashville: Thomas Nelson, 1980) is a
comprehensive handbook of the people of the Bible and
how they lived. Its photographs of terrain, ruins, plants,
and archaeological discoveries are invaluable.

Some of its chapter titles are "Pagan Religions and
Cultures," "The Egyptians," "The Persians," "The Minerals
and Gems of Palestine," "Transportation," and "Warfare
and Weapons."

Halley's Bible Handbook by Henry H. Halley (Grand Rapids:
Zondervan Publishing House, 1965) is an abbreviated
Bible commentary arranged according to the books of the
Bible. It contains general notes and insights on practically

every chapter of the Old and New Testaments. It is designed for the Bible reader who has few commentaries or reference works, but many Bible scholars find it helpful.

The New American Standard Exhaustive Concordance of the Bible (Nashville: Holman, 1981) was my source for Hebrew word definitions.

The Pictorial Bible Dictionary edited by Merrill C. Tenney (Franklin, Tenn.: Southwestern Company, 1975). I have found this work especially helpful. It is very readable and surprisingly complete for a one-volume work. It includes more than five thousand entries and contains the work of sixty-five competent scholars in every field from archaeology to zoology.

Theological Wordbook of the Old Testament by R. Laird Harris, Gleason L. Archer, and Bruce K. Waltke (Chicago: Moody Press, 1980) is an excellent source for more extensive word studies.